Presented to:

_____

Gift of the Riverside
Community Development
Block Grant

The
Peacock's
Pride

MELISSA KAJPUST

ILLUSTRATED BY JO'ANNE KELLY

Hyperion Books for Children
New York

For Kendra and Brenna —M.K.

The author gratefully acknowledges the assistance of the following people:
Dr. Klostermaier, Dr. Hadi Husain, Philip King, Rubena Sinha, Nanditta Biswas, and
Clive Roots. A special thanks to my friends at Beausejour Elementary School.

Text © 1997 by Melissa Kajpust.
Illustrations © 1997 by Jo'Anne Kelly.

Printed in Hong Kong.
Designed by A. O. Osen.

FIRST EDITION
10 9 8 7 6 5 4 3 2 1

Library of Congress Cataloging-In-Publication Data
Kajpust, Melissa.
       The peacock's pride / [retold] by Melissa Kajpust : illustrated by Jo'Anne Kelly.–1st ed.
          p.   cm.
       Summary: A retelling of a traditional tale from northern India in which a conceited peacock
learns that beauty has many forms.
       ISBN 0-7868-0293-6 (trade)—ISBN 0-7868-2233-3 (lib. bdg.)
       [1. Folklore—India. 2. Peacock—Folklore.] I. Kelly, Jo'Anne. ill. II. Title.
PZ8.1.K1275Pe 1997
398.2'0954'4528617–dc20   96-33664

The illustrations are prepared using watercolor and gouache.
This book is set in 14-point New Baskerville BE.

One day, long ago, Peacock strutted through the forest with his royal blue crown held high. In the flickering light, his long back feathers created a magnificent blue-green fan that shimmered like sapphires and emeralds. He stopped beneath a banyan tree that grew near a water hole and turned his heavy plumage slowly, hoping to attract the admiration of a group of birds sitting on the branches above him. But the birds had more immediate concerns.

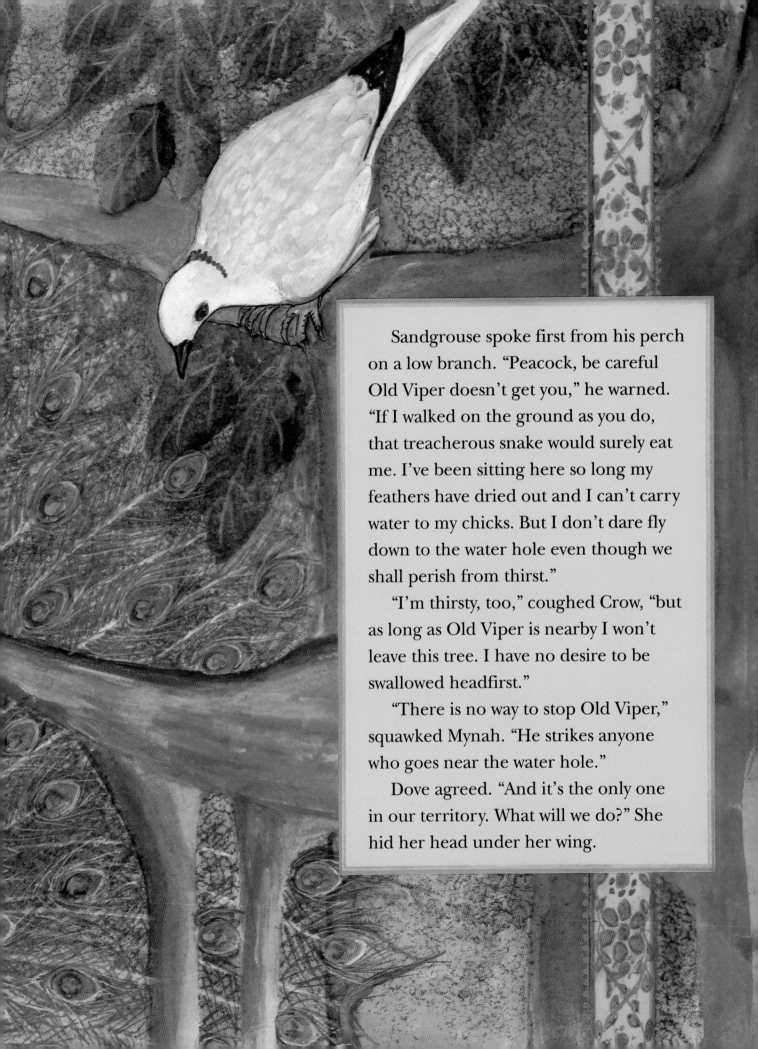

Sandgrouse spoke first from his perch on a low branch. "Peacock, be careful Old Viper doesn't get you," he warned. "If I walked on the ground as you do, that treacherous snake would surely eat me. I've been sitting here so long my feathers have dried out and I can't carry water to my chicks. But I don't dare fly down to the water hole even though we shall perish from thirst."

"I'm thirsty, too," coughed Crow, "but as long as Old Viper is nearby I won't leave this tree. I have no desire to be swallowed headfirst."

"There is no way to stop Old Viper," squawked Mynah. "He strikes anyone who goes near the water hole."

Dove agreed. "And it's the only one in our territory. What will we do?" She hid her head under her wing.

The birds continued to fret and complain. Peacock became annoyed that no one was paying attention to him. He turned his head to gaze at the assembled creatures. They are all rather plain, he thought, and so noisy and undignified. I must devise a plan to rid them of this troublesome snake so they can give me the praise and attention I deserve.

After some thought he said, "You need not concern yourselves with Old Viper any longer. My hypnotic beauty will easily defeat him."

"Beauty is no match for Old Viper's deadly venom," Mynah said, unimpressed.

The others murmured agreement, thinking Peacock both conceited and foolish.

"My feathers have great powers." Peacock replied. "My fan has a thousand magic eyes that will stare Old Viper into a trance. I'll then seize him by the neck and kill him. You will be rid of him forever."

"It sounds like a good plan," Sandgrouse agreed. "But why would you do this for us?"

Peacock smiled slyly, angling his fan so that it flashed brilliantly. "If I succeed, everyone must acknowledge me king of the water hole."

The birds held a hasty conference. "It's true that Peacock has countless eyes," Dove observed. "Perhaps he knows things we don't. What harm can it do to call him king?"

Sandgrouse was skeptical, but because they were all so thirsty they finally agreed to Peacock's plan. As the birds watched from the safety of the tree, Peacock approached the water hole and began to drink.

Immediately Old Viper slithered from behind a log.

"Look out behind you," Mynah shrieked.

Peacock turned so that Old Viper could have the full effect of his feathers. His fan's eyes focused on the snake, who was caught in its unblinking stare. His head lowered, Old Viper flicked his tongue in and out, and soon the vicious animal fell into a trance. Peacock quickly pinned the snake down with his claw and killed him with his beak.

A joyful cackle arose from the banyan tree! The birds flew down from their perches and drank greedily at the water hole. Everyone praised Peacock's beauty and power. They all exclaimed that he was certainly worthy of being king.

As the weeks passed, Peacock spent all his time strutting around the water hole and gazing adoringly at his reflection in the water. Why should I have to do anything for myself? he thought. After all, I am the king. "Mynah," Peacock commanded, "from now on you must preen my feathers until they shine like dew-wet leaves."

Mynah grumbled but did as she was asked. Then Peacock announced, "The banks of the water hole are too muddy for my walks. Sandgrouse, you must fetch my drinking water. And Dove must fan me with her wings so that I stay cool and comfortable."

One day while Peacock was parading along the forest path, the other birds gathered at the banyan tree. "Peacock allows us to drink only when he is away from the water hole. He is as oppressive as Old Viper was," Sandgrouse complained.

"He makes me bring him all his food," Crow said. "I have no time to sit on my eggs."

"We are still prisoners," concluded Mynah. "We must *now* rid ourselves of Peacock!"

While they were talking Koel came to the water hole and overheard their conversation.

This plain, black bird had no distinguishing features. Timid, he usually kept to himself. Today he spoke. "Excuse me," he said, "but I know how to solve this problem. We must teach Peacock a lesson. We must challenge the power of his great beauty with something even more beautiful. If you like, I will make this challenge."

"I don't mean to be rude," said Mynah, staring at the shy bird with its dull coat and thin tail. "But what makes you think you can solve our problem?"

"I have a plan," said Koel, who knew a great deal about peacocks.

That afternoon Koel approached Peacock. "You have the most beautiful feathers I have ever seen," he said. "I am wondering if I too have a gift equal to your beauty?"

Peacock stared at the dowdy creature. He could hardly suppress his laughter.

"Would you agree," Koel continued, "to give up your kingdom if I can prove that my beauty is every bit as great as yours?"

Peacock readily agreed. How could this small, drab-looking bird ever hope to match his splendor?

Immediately Koel flapped to a branch of the banyan tree and poured forth a remarkable song. His voice was so clear and sweet, its notes so thrilling, that all the forest grew still. Even Peacock was amazed by the grace and beauty of Koel's song.

"You do indeed possess a remarkably lovely voice," Peacock said. "And I admit that it is as beautiful as my feathers. But I have a voice, too. I'm sure that my song will be every bit as wonderful."

Koel smiled confidently, but the other birds were worried. They had never heard Peacock sing so they did not know what to expect. Crow knew that her noisy caw would never win any singing contest. Dove's soft *du-du-du* put the other birds to sleep. Mynah squawked and Sandgrouse clucked. Since Peacock was so much more beautiful than they, surely his voice must be equally outstanding.

Peacock took a deep breath, tilted his head, and began his song. *"Minh-ao, minh-ao,"* he yelled as if in terrible pain. He tried again. *"Minh-ao, minh-ao!"* His two-note shriek filled the air.

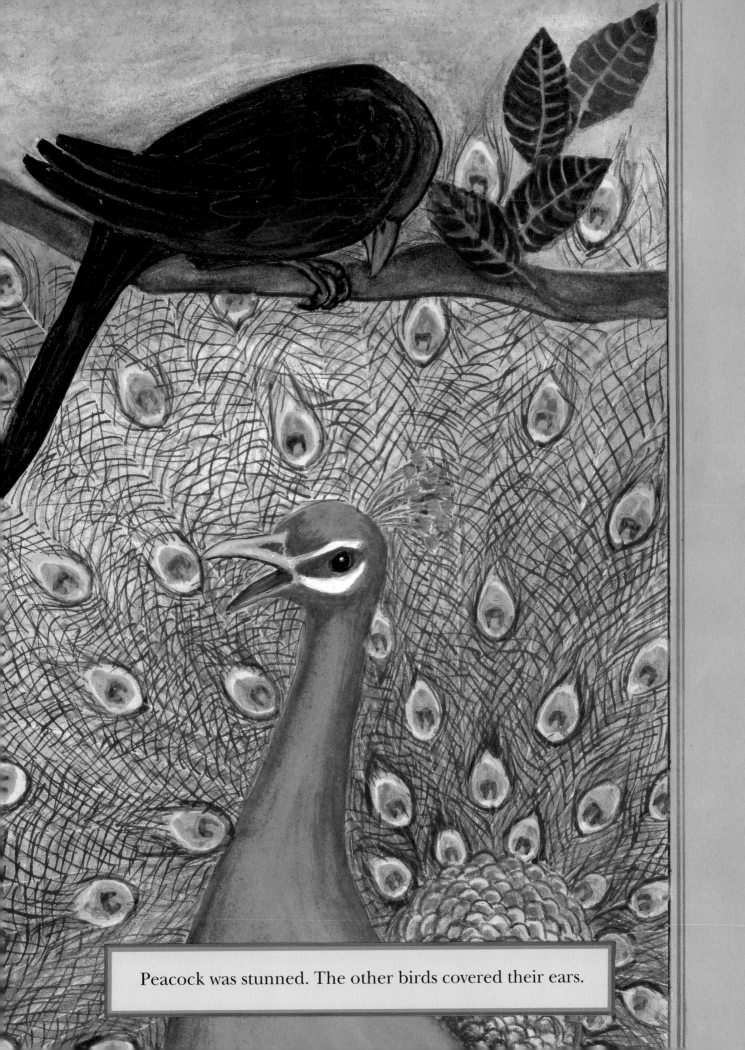

Peacock was stunned. The other birds covered their ears.

Peacock knew that he had been defeated. Slowly he folded his magnificent feathers until the shimmering blue and green fan disappeared. Koel graciously praised Peacock. "You are indeed uniquely beautiful, but each of us is special in our own way," he said.

And that is how Peacock came to drag his train of feathers behind him, no longer blinded with pride.

Author's Note

The India blue wild peafowl, more commonly known as the peacock, is the national bird of India. It is the oldest and most flamboyant ornamental bird known to man. The male has a six- to eight-foot train made from the long feathers on its back and supported by shorter tail feathers. The fronds of each feather are green, patterned with a gold, blue, and black "eye" at the tip. When all the feathers are spread, the effect is of dozens of eyes gazing at the viewer. Balancing the raised "fan" shifts the bird's normal walking gait into a strut and may be responsible for its reputation of pride. The bird's great beauty is in stark contrast to its raucous, shrieking voice.

The koel is a member of the cuckoo family. Although both the male and female sing, the male is better known for its glorious song. It is often described as the nightingale of India.

Indian folktales deal with everyday life. Animal characters are given human traits, and the stories deal with daily relationships and personality characteristics. Usually the character that triumphs is the hardworking underdog. Morally superior but humble characters most often succeed. Truthfulness, modesty, loyalty, courage, generosity, and honest effort are greatly valued. In India, folktales are handed down through the generations and represent an important moral tradition in Indian culture.

This story comes from northern India and is based on common folklore. There are many reputed sources for the power of the eyes on the peacock's feathers. According to one Hindu legend, Indra, the god of thunder, rain, and war, was changed into a peacock in order to escape the demon Ravana. As compensation, the peacock was endowed with a thousand eyes in his feathers. Peacocks are allowed to wander freely in gardens because the eyes are said to possess hypnotic powers over serpents, which enables the peacock to kill them. The power of the eyes is thought to affect peahens as well, who become entranced by the eyes during mating season.